THE WILLOWISP

Christmas Book

Published by Willowisp Press, Inc.
401 E. Wilson Bridge Road, Worthington, Ohio 43085

Printed in the United States of America
10 9 8 7 6 5 4 3 2 1

ISBN 0-87406-408-2

Contents

Introduction

Welcome to *The Willowisp Christmas Book.* Everything in it has been chosen to help you experience the magic of the most wonderful time of the year. You can read about the very first Christmas, so long ago. You can learn the stories behind your favorite Christmas symbols and traditions. You can read how people all over the world celebrate the holiday. You can even learn to make your own Christmas gifts, decorations, and treats! On top of all this, *The Willowisp Christmas Book* contains many of the best-loved stories and poems that make this time of the year so special.

Christmas is a time of sharing. We know you'll want to share *The Willowisp Christmas Book* with your family and friends. Read some of the stories and poems out loud to your family. Tell your friends about other countries' holiday customs. We hope that your new book will become a part of your very own Christmas tradition.

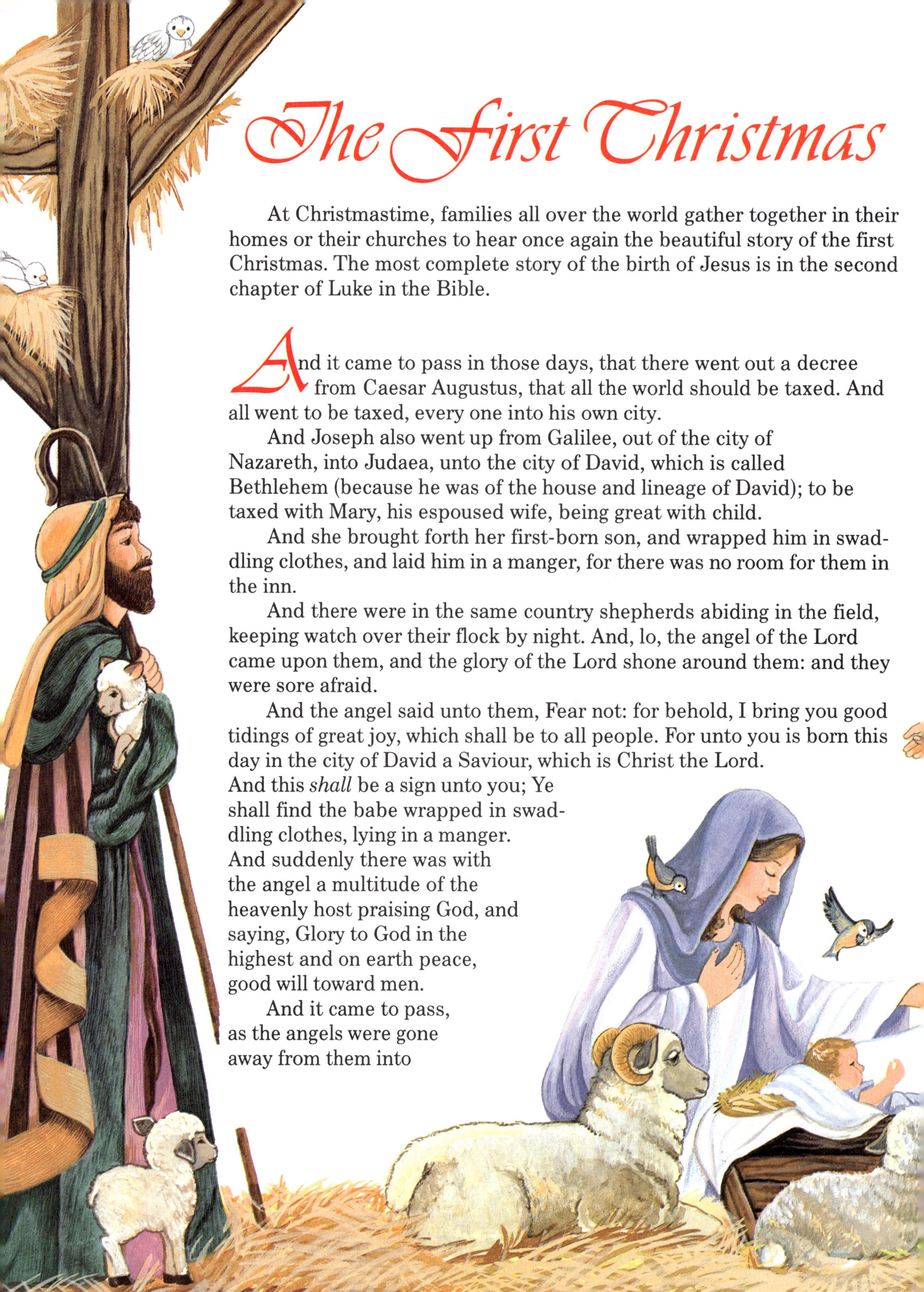

The First Christmas

At Christmastime, families all over the world gather together in their homes or their churches to hear once again the beautiful story of the first Christmas. The most complete story of the birth of Jesus is in the second chapter of Luke in the Bible.

And it came to pass in those days, that there went out a decree from Caesar Augustus, that all the world should be taxed. And all went to be taxed, every one into his own city.

And Joseph also went up from Galilee, out of the city of Nazareth, into Judaea, unto the city of David, which is called Bethlehem (because he was of the house and lineage of David); to be taxed with Mary, his espoused wife, being great with child.

And she brought forth her first-born son, and wrapped him in swaddling clothes, and laid him in a manger, for there was no room for them in the inn.

And there were in the same country shepherds abiding in the field, keeping watch over their flock by night. And, lo, the angel of the Lord came upon them, and the glory of the Lord shone around them: and they were sore afraid.

And the angel said unto them, Fear not: for behold, I bring you good tidings of great joy, which shall be to all people. For unto you is born this day in the city of David a Saviour, which is Christ the Lord. And this *shall* be a sign unto you; Ye shall find the babe wrapped in swaddling clothes, lying in a manger. And suddenly there was with the angel a multitude of the heavenly host praising God, and saying, Glory to God in the highest and on earth peace, good will toward men.

And it came to pass, as the angels were gone away from them into

heaven, the shepherds said one to another, Let us now go even unto Bethlehem, and see this thing which is come to pass, which the Lord hath made known to us. And they came with haste, and found Mary, and Joseph, and the babe lying in the manger.

What Child Is This?

This old English carol is sung to the famous tune "Greensleeves." It contrasts the humble birth of Jesus in the stable with his later glory as the King of Kings.

What child is this who, laid to rest,
On Mary's lap is sleeping?
Whom angels greet with anthems sweet
While shepherds watch are keeping?
This, this is Christ the King
Whom shepherds guard and angels sing;
Haste, haste to bring him laud,
The Babe, the Son of Mary!

Why lies He in such mean estate,
Where ox and ass are feeding?
Good Christians, fear; for sinners here
The silent Word is pleading.
Nails, spear shall pierce Him through,
The Cross be borne for me, for you;
Hail, hail, the Word made flesh,
The Babe, the Son of Mary!

So bring Him incense, gold, and myrrh,
Come, peasant, king, to worship Him;
The King of Kings salvation brings:
Let loving hearts enthrone Him.
Raise, raise the song on high,
The Virgin sings her lullaby:
Joy, joy for Christ is born,
The Babe, the Son of Mary!

Christmas Dance at Mr. Fezziwig's

from *A Christmas Carol* by Charles Dickens

Nobody has described the joys of Christmas better than the English author Charles Dickens. His tale of old Ebenezer Scrooge, Tiny Tim, and the ghosts of Christmas is a favorite throughout the world. Here Dickens describes the Christmas party of Mr. Fezziwig, a kind old gentleman.

"Yo ho, my boys!" said Fezziwig. "No more work tonight. Christmas Eve. Let's have the shutters up," cried old Fezziwig, with a sharp clap of his hands, "before a man can say, Jack Robinson!"

"Hilli-ho!" cried old Fezziwig. "Clear away my lads, and let's have lots of room here!"

Clear away! There was nothing they wouldn't have cleared away, or couldn't have cleared away, with old Fezziwig looking on. It was done in a minute. Every movable was packed off, as if it were dismissed from public life for evermore; the floor was swept and watered, the lamps were trimmed, fuel was heaped upon the fire, and the warehouse was as snug, and warm, and dry, and bright as a ball-room as you would desire to see on a winter's night.

In came a fiddler with a music book, and went up to a lofty desk, and made an orchestra of it, and tuned like fifty stomach-aches. In came Mrs. Fezziwig, one vast substantial smile. In came the three Miss Fezziwigs, beaming and lovable. In came the six young followers whose hearts they broke. In came all the young men and women employed in the business. In came the housemaid, with her cousin the baker. In came the cook, with her brother's particular friend, the milkman. In they all came, one after another; some shyly, some boldly, some gracefully, some awkwardly, some pushing, some pulling; in they all came, anyhow and everyhow. Away they all went, twenty couple at once, hands half round and back again the other way; down the middle and up again; round and round in various stages of affectionate grouping; old top couple always turning up in the wrong place; new top couple starting off again, as soon as they got there; all top couples at last, and not a bottom one to help them. When this result was brought about, old Fezziwig, clapping his hands to stop the dance, cried out, "Well done!"

Christmas Symbols and Traditions

Everywhere you look at this happy time of the year, you see symbols of Christmas. How did all our symbols and traditions become a part of Christmas?

The Christmas Tree

For most people, Christmas wouldn't be Christmas without a beautiful tree, covered with lights and special ornaments. Where does this tradition come from? And how did it get to be the most popular Christmas symbol?

In the Middle Ages, people brought cut evergreen trees and boughs into their houses in the middle of winter. The green branches reminded them that life continued, even in the deep, dark winter months. They felt that the branches also frightened away demons and evil spirits, something we don't worry too much about today.

People in Germany began to decorate the trees with pretty objects, candles, and special foods. The custom soon spread to other parts of the world, including North America.

Today, many families enjoy cutting their own tree at a tree farm. Some people even buy live trees to decorate at Christmas. Then they plant the trees in the spring and enjoy them the year round.

The Manger Scene

Many homes celebrate the Christmas season by setting up a manger scene, sometimes called a creche (pronounced *kresh*). It's fun to look at the different figures in a creche—the shepherds and their animals, the wise men, the angels, Mary and Joseph, and the baby Jesus in his cradle. What would it be like to be born in an animal stall? How would you have felt if you were one of the shepherds there at the manger long ago?

The first creche was made by St. Francis of Assisi in 1223. Like some churches do today, he used live people and animals. Have you ever been in a live manger scene?

Poinsettias

Beautiful red poinsettias are a part of Christmas in lots of homes. They were named for Dr. Joel Roberts Poinsett, the first U.S. ambassador to Mexico. He introduced the plant to the U.S. in about 1830. The star shape of its leaves is a reminder of the Star of Bethlehem that led the wise men to the manger.

Santa Claus

When we hear sleigh bells, reindeer hooves on the roof, and a jolly laugh, it means only one thing—Santa Claus is coming to town! But did you know that he hasn't always looked the way he does today?

The name Santa Claus comes from Saint Nicholas, an early Christian saint who was known as the protector of children. Dutch children believed that Saint Nicholas was the Christmas Man who filled their wooden shoes with presents on Christmas Eve. They called him Sinter Klaas. He was tall and thin and dressed like a church bishop. And he rode a white horse.

The Dutch brought Sinter Klaas to North America, where he became mixed up with the Christmas traditions and legends of many other countries. He also grew a long white beard, found some reindeer, and got a whole lot fatter! But he's still the symbol of good will and generosity that all children love.

Christmas Cards

Compared to many Christmas traditions that date back thousands of years, sending cards is a new custom. One of the first people to send Christmas cards was Queen Victoria of England's printer in the 1840s. The queen thought it was a nice idea and soon started sending them to her friends. After that, the custom of sending Christmas cards spread around the world.

Gifts

Have you ever gotten gold, frankincense, or myrrh for Christmas? Probably not. But when we give and receive gifts today, we remember the gifts of the three wise men to the baby Jesus.

Christmas Carols

Christmas just wouldn't be the same without all our beautiful carols. Some carols are as old as ancient Roman times, and some were just written last year. The word carol is very old, but it didn't come to mean a Christmas song until the 1400s. Before then a carol was just a kind of dance.

Now people all over the world love to get together at Christmastime and sing their favorite carols. What's your favorite Christmas carol?

Stockings

Old Saint Nicholas also started the tradition of hanging stockings at Christmas. He was a busy man! The legend says that once he heard about three sisters who were too poor to get married. He felt sorry for them and dropped some gold pieces down their chimney. The gold landed in stockings that the sisters had hung on the fireplace to dry! That's why we hang out our stockings on Christmas Eve for Santa Claus to fill.

Christmas at Mole's House

from *The Wind in the Willows* by Kenneth Grahame

Have you ever read this all-time favorite? It tells the story of Rat, Mole, Badger, and the wild and wacky Toad, who live by the river. In this episode, Rat and Mole have just returned to Mole's little hole in the ground (which is really more like a very cozy cottage!). The carol that the field-mice sing tells how it was the animals at the manger who were the first ones to praise the baby Jesus. Mole and Rat are fixing a snack when they hear voices outside.

"What's up?" inquired the Rat, pausing in his labours.

"I think it must be the field-mice," replied the mole, with a touch of pride in his manner. "They go round carol-singing regularly at this time of the year. And they never pass me over—they come to Mole End last of all; and I used to give them hot drinks, and supper too sometimes, when I could afford it. It will be like old times to hear them again."

"Let's have a look at them!" cried the Rat, jumping up and running to the door.

It was a pretty sight, and a seasonable one, that met their eyes when they flung the door open. In the forecourt, lit by the dim rays of a horn lantern, some eight or ten little field-mice stood in a semicircle, red worsted comforters round their throats, their forepaws thrust deep into their pockets, their feet jigging for warmth. With bright beady eyes, they glanced shyly at each other, sniggering a little, sniffing and applying coat-sleeves a good deal. As the door opened, one of the elder ones that carried the lantern was just saying, "Now then, one, two, three!" and forthwith their shrill little voices uprose on the air, singing one of the old-time carols that their forefathers composed in the fields that were fallow and held by frost, or when snow-bound in chimney corners, and handed down to be sung in the miry streets to lamplit windows at Yule-time.

Carols

Villagers all, this frosty tide,
Let your doors swing open wide,
Though wind may follow, and snow
—beside,
Yet draw us in by your fire to bide;
Joy shall be yours in the morning!

Here we stand in the cold and the sleet,
Blowing fingers and stamping feet,
Come from far away you to greet—
You by the fire and we in the street—
Bidding you joy in the morning!

For ere one half of the night was gone,
Sudden a star has led us on,
Raining bliss and benison*—
Bliss to-morrow and more anon,
Joy for every morning!

Goodman Joseph toiled through
the snow—
Saw the star o'er a stable low;
Mary she might not further go—
Welcome thatch and litter below!
Joy was hers in the morning!

And when they heard the angels tell
'Who were the first to cry Nowell?
Animals all, as it befell,
In the stable where they did dwell!
Joy shall be theirs in the
morning!

The voices ceased, the singers, bashful but smiling, exchanged sidelong glances, and silence succeeded—but for a moment only. Then, from up above and far away, down the tunnel they had so lately travelled was borne to their ears in a faint musical hum the sound of distant bells ringing a joyful and clangorous peal.

"Very well sung, boys!" cried the Rat heartily. "And now come along in, all of you, and warm yourselves by the fire, and have something hot!"

*blessing

Christmas Around the World

All around the world, the reason for celebrating Christmas is the same—the birth of Jesus. But each country has its own special way of celebrating the holiday. Let's take a journey through the wonderful world of Christmas!

England

Families go to a Christmas Eve midnight church service. That night, Father Christmas leaves small presents for good children. The day after Christmas is called Boxing Day. On this day, churches used to set out boxes to collect money for poor people. Some people also think the name comes from the old custom of giving gifts in boxes to servants and workers.

Christmas dinner in England has always been a fabulous feast. The traditional dishes used to be boar's (wild pig) head and roasted peacock! But now families usually eat goose, roast beef or turkey. The meal is still finished with the famous plum pudding, blazing with brandy!

Scotland

Christmas in Scotland is usually a quiet, family affair. But anyone leaving the house on Christmas Day must remember to bring a gift if he plans to return to the house during the day. On Christmas Eve, Scots bake round cakes flavored with caraway seeds for each family member. But they have to be careful with their cakes. It's bad luck if the cake breaks.

Ireland

If you were in Ireland at Christmastime, you'd see lighted candles in almost every window. The candles guide people who, like Mary and Joseph, are looking for shelter.

December 26 is called Saint Stephen's Day. On this day, you might see a tradition called the Feeding of the Wren. Boys catch a wren bird and put it in a cage. They carry the cage from door to door collecting money for the bird.

United States and Canada

The Christmas season in the United States begins on Thanksgiving Day, the fourth Thursday in November. On that day in many large cities, giant holiday parades attract thousands of people. Santa Claus himself always appears on a beautiful float at the end of the parade.

Many American and Canadian families go to Christmas Eve church service and exchange presents that evening or the next morning. Of course, Santa Claus makes his visit on Christmas Eve, leaving gifts under the tree or in the stockings.

In addition to these customs many Canadians and Americans have special traditions. In Quebec, the French-speaking part of Canada, people have kept many Christmas traditions from France. In the southwestern U.S., Mexican traditions are strong. And many black families combine Christmas celebrations with an Afro-American holiday called *Kwanzaa.*

France

If you were a French boy or girl, you'd leave your shoes by the fireplace for *Pere Noel* (Father Christmas) to fill with presents. But watch out for his helper. He's *Pere Fouettard* (Father Spanker). Guess what he does to children who haven't been good!

The Yule log is a popular tradition in France. The whole family selects a tree, and the father and oldest son cut it down. They carry the huge log into the house, walk around the room three times with it, and then place it in the fireplace. The family pours a glass of wine on the log and sings Christmas songs.

Germany

The most important German tradition is Tannenbaum—the Christmas tree. It has spread all over the world. But in some German families, the mother often decoratesTannenbaum in secret. She reveals the tree on Christmas Eve.

German children look forward to the visit of Saint Nicholas. In some parts of Germany, Saint Nicholas collects wish-lists from children and gives them to the *Christkindl* (the Christ child). The Christkindl brings presents on Christmas Eve. In other parts of Germany, Saint Nicholas brings a helper, Prince Ruprecht, who carries a sack. But the Prince's sack is empty. And into it go naughty children!

Greece

Greek families have to be very careful throughout the holiday season, but especially on Christmas Eve. That's when *Kallikantzaroi* are roaming around. They are monsters with large heads and hairy bodies who break into houses and do all kinds of nasty things. They eat the Christmas food the family has been saving. They smash the furniture. Families can hang sweets and sausages in the fireplace for the monsters to eat. If this doesn't work, they have to get a priest to bless the house and chase away the monsters!

Australia

There won't ever be a white Christmas in Australia. That's because Christmas arrives in the middle of summer! But people can go to the beach and have a picnic on Christmas Day,

and that's what lots of Australians do.

The Christmas tree is different in Australia, too. Many people have a Christmas bush, a plant with clusters of tiny soft flowers that grows in Australia.

Italy

Christmas trees aren't common in Italy. Instead, the *presepio*, or a creche scene, is at the center of the Italian Christmas. But not until Christmas Eve does the holy *Bambino* appear in the crib!

Italian children believe in an old woman named Saint Befana, who comes down the chimney and fills the shoes of good children with presents. Parents threaten to tell Befana when a child is bad. Then she'll fill the bad child's shoes with ashes!

Do you love spaghetti? Then maybe you'd like to celebrate Christmas in Italy someday. Spaghetti is part of the Christmas meal in some parts of Italy. And how do you feel about eating eel? That's on the menu, too.

Mexico

You've probably seen, or even made, one of the most important Mexican Christmas traditions. It's the *piñata,* a clay or papier mâché pot in the shape of a bird or animal and covered with tissue paper. Mexicans fill the *piñata* with small candies, toys, nuts, and souvenirs and hang it from the ceiling. Blindfolded children take turns trying to swat the swinging *piñata* and break it open, scattering its treasures all over the floor.

The *piñata* is an old Aztec Indian custom, a sacrifice to the war god *Haizilopochtli*. Early Catholic missionaries adapted this tradition to the celebration of the Christmas season.

Sweden

This cold, snowy, northern country has one of the most beautiful Christmas traditions. December 13 is Saint Lucia's Day, the start of the Swedish Christmas season. The oldest daughter in a home represents Saint Lucia, the saint of light. She wears a crown of candles and a white gown and wakes her family with coffee, buns, and cookies. Saint Lucia pageants all over Sweden bring hope and light to the coldest, dreariest time of the year.

"Merry Christmas" in Different Languages

No matter how you say it, it all means just one thing!

French—Joyeux Noel
German—Frœhliche Weinachten
Spanish—Felices Pascuas, Feliz Navidad
Danish—Glaedelig Jul
Dutch—Zalig Kerstfeest
Finnish—Hauskaa Joulua
Italian—Buon Natale
Portuguese—Boas Festas
Swedish—God Jul
Chinese—Kung Hsi Hsin Nien bing Chu Shen Tan
Irish—Nollaig faoi shean agus faoi shonas duit
Russian—S Rozhdestvom Kristovym
Turkish—Noeliniz kutlu olsun
Polish—Wesolych Swiat

A Visit from St. Nicholas

by Clement Moore

The most famous Christmas poem of all was published anonymously in the *Troy* (New York) *Sentinel* on December 23, 1823. The author didn't think it was good enough to put his name on it.

Twas the night before Christmas, when all through the house
Not a creature was stirring, not even a mouse;
The stockings were hung by the chimney with care,
In hopes that St. Nicholas soon would be there;
The children were nestled all snug in their beds,
While visions of sugar-plums danced in their heads;
And mamma in her kerchief and I in my cap
Had just settled our brains for a long winter's nap,
When out on the lawn there arose such a clatter,
I sprang from my bed to see what was the matter.
Away to the window I flew like a flash,
Tore open the shutters, and threw up the sash;
The moon, on the breast of the new-fallen snow,
Gave a lustre of midday to objects below;
When what to my wondering eyes should appear
But a miniature sleigh and eight tiny reindeer,
With a little old driver, so lively and quick,

I knew in a moment, it must be St. Nick.
More rapid than eagles his coursers they came,
And he whistled and shouted and called them by name:
"Now Dasher! now Dancer!
now Prancer! now Vixen!
On, Comet! on, Cupid! on, Donder and Blitzen!
To the top of the porch! To the top of the wall!
Now, dash away, dash away, dash away, all!"
As dry leaves that before the wild hurricane fly,
When they meet with an obstacle, mount to the sky,
So up to the housetop the coursers they flew,
With the sleigh full of toys and St. Nicholas too.
And then, in a twinkling, I heard on the roof
The prancing and pawing of each little hoof.
As I drew in my head and was turning around,
Down the chimney St. Nicholas came with a bound.
He was dressed all in fur, from his head to his foot,
And his clothes were all tarnished with ashes and soot;
A bundle of toys he had flung on his back,
And he looked like a peddler just opening his pack.
His eyes: how they twinkled! his dimples: how merry!
His cheeks were like roses, his nose like a cherry;
His droll little mouth was drawn up like a bow,
And the beard on his chin was as white as the snow.
The stump of a pipe he held tight in his teeth,
And the smoke, it encircled his head like a wreath:
He had a broad face, and a little round belly,
That shook, when he laughed, like a bowl full of jelly;
He was chubby and plump, a right jolly old elf;
And I laughed, when I saw him, in spite of myself,
A wink of his eye and a twist of his head
Soon gave me to know I had nothing to dread.
He spoke not a word, but went straight to his work,
And filled all the stockings; then turned with a jerk,
And laying his finger aside of his nose,
And giving a nod, up the chimney he rose.
He sprang to his sleigh, to his team gave a whistle,
And away they all flew like the down of a thistle;
But I heard him exclaim, ere he drove out of sight,
"Happy Christmas to all, and to all a good-night!"

Yes, Virginia, There Is a Santa Claus

from the *New York Sun,* September 21, 1897

Almost a hundred years ago, a young girl wrote this letter to a newspaper. The answer, written by Francis Pharcellus Church, has become a Christmas classic.

Dear Editor—I am 8 years old. Some of my little friends say there is no Santa Claus. Papa says, "If you see it in the *Sun*, it's so." Please tell me the truth, is there a Santa Claus?

Virginia O'Hanlon

Yes, Virginia, there is a Santa Claus. He exists as certainly as love and generosity and devotion exists, and you know that they abound and give to your life its highest beauty and joy. Alas! how dreary would be the world if there were no Santa Claus! It would be as dreary as if there were no Virginias. There would be no childlike faith then, no poetry, no romance to make tolerable this existence. We should have no enjoyment, except in sense and sight. The eternal light with which childhood fills the world would be extinguished.

Not believe in Santa Claus! You might as well not believe in fairies! You might get your papa to hire men to watch in all the chimneys on Christmas Eve to catch Santa Claus, but even if they did not see Santa Claus coming down, what would that prove? Nobody sees Santa Claus, but that is no sign that there is no Santa Claus. The most real things in the world are those that neither children nor men can see. Did you ever see fairies dancing on the lawn? Of course not, but that's no proof that they are not there. Nobody can conceive or imagine all the wonders there are unseen and unseeable in the world.

... No Santa Claus! Thank God! he lives, and he lives forever. A thousand years from now, Virginia, nay ten times ten thousand years from now, he will continue to make glad the heart of childhood.

Christmas Gifts, Decorations, Cards and Foods You Can Make Yourself

Walking around in stores or watching TV commercials at Christmastime might make you think that you need a ton of money to celebrate the holiday. But sometimes, the most special gift is the one that you make yourself.

There are lots of fantastic gifts you can make for practically nothing. And they'll be special because they're made by you. Nobody could buy them for any amount of money. And that will make the person who receives your gift feel special, too.

This section also has ideas for other great Christmas projects you can do yourself. Try to think up some of your own ideas, too.

Have a Merry Home-made Christmas!

Jigsaw Puzzle

What you'll need: paste, cardboard, scissors, a photo (it can be of your parents, of you or your brothers and sisters, or even of your pet)

Paste the photo onto the cardboard. After it dries, cut it into different-shaped pieces.

Place Mats

What you'll need: a picture that you've drawn or one that you've cut from a magazine, clear plastic with adhesive backing

Cover both sides of the drawing or picture with the plastic. Make enough placemats so each member of the family can have one. If the placemats get dirty, just wipe them clean with a wet dish cloth.

Napkin Rings

(These can go with the placemats.)
What you'll need: needle and thread, red and green and whatever other kinds of felt you want, pinking shears or scissors, fabric glue, glitter or sequins

Cut the felt into1-1/2-inch (4 cm) by 7-inch (18 cm) strips. Sew the ends together to form a ring, overlapping about an inch (2-1/2 cm). (Be careful with the needle. Don't find out the hard way how sharp it is!) Glue the glitter, sequins, or felt onto the ring. You could use red and green felt and cut Christmas trees out of the green felt to glue onto the red ring. Or, spread glue on the ring and sprinkle glitter on the glue. Use your imagination, and don't forget to make enough rings for everybody in your family.

Gift Certificates

Parents will really appreciate these!

What you'll need: index cards, hole punch, markers, yarn

Punch holes every few inches all around the edge of an index card. Weave a piece of yarn in and out of the holes and tie it in a bow on the top or bottom of the card. Write "To" and then a line at the top. Finish the gift certificate by writing things like:

I will clean my room every Saturday for a month.

I will help clear dishes from the dinner table every day for a week.

This coupon entitles you to 10 hugs.

I will shovel snow three times this winter (or rake leaves, cut the grass, clean the garage).

Hint: practice writing the message once on another piece of paper. Then it will be neater when you write it on the gift certificate. Be sure to sign your name to the bottom of each card.

Stone Paperweights

Keep your eyes open throughout the year for neat rocks and stones. Grab them, and put them in a safe place. You can use them to make a fun and useful gift for someone for Christmas. And it'll be funny to watch people try to guess what's in the heavy package—don't tell!

What you'll need: glue, paint, glitter, clean stones

Glue the stones together. (Hint: arrange them in different ways before you start

gluing. This way you can find the neatest combinations.) Glue enough stones together so the paperweight is about as big as your fist. Let the glue dry, and paint the stones. Or, if the rocks look pretty just as they are, don't paint them. Leave them natural!

Ornaments

Homemade ornaments always look great on your Christmas tree. They're one-of-a-kind. No other tree in the world will have ornaments exactly like yours. Here are a few you might want to try.

Personalized Christmas Balls

What you'll need: plain glass Christmas balls, glue, glitter

Spell out a person's name on the balls with glue. Sprinkle glitter on the ball. The glitter will stick to the glue, and you'll have an ornament with a person's name on it. Be sure to do this over a piece of newspaper so the glitter doesn't get all over the floor.

Noodle Ornaments

These really look fabulous on a dark green tree!

What you'll need: paper plates or cardboard, macaroni of different shapes and sizes, white glue, gold or silver spray paint, scissors, yarn, hole punch, newspaper

Cut stars, circles, bells, or other Christmas shapes from the cardboard or paper plates. The shapes should be about 3 inches (8 cm) wide. Make sure you have two of each cardboard shape that are exactly alike. Hold the matching ones together and punch holes in the tops so they line up. Glue the macaroni to one side of each shape, and let it dry.

On the newspaper, spray paint the noodle sides of the shapes, and let them dry. Glue the front and back pieces together, and tie a piece of yarn through the hole.

Quick Stained Glass Ornament

These are fragile. You might not want to put them on the tree because they might get poked. Hang them in a window instead.

What you'll need: black yarn, wax paper, white glue, marking pens

Lay the wax paper flat. Arrange the yarn in a circle, and continue arranging it in twists and curves inside the circle. Stick a loop of yarn out the top of the circle. Fill the circle up with the glue to the top of the yarn. Don't worry—white glue dries clear. When the glue is dry, use marking pens to fill in the clear area. Pull off the wax paper, and hang your ornament in a window so the sun can shine through it.

God's Eyes

These beautiful ornaments come from the Indians of the American Southwest. Use your imagination to put together any designs you want.

What you'll need: Red and green and any other colors of yarn you want, pipe cleaners, scissors

Twist the pipe cleaners together to form an *X*. Tie one end of the red yarn to the center of the *X*. Now wrap the yarn over and under the arms of the *X*. To make a different design, just tie the end of the red yarn to the end of the green yarn and keep wrapping all the way to the ends of the *X*. You can snip off the ends of the knot later. Make a loop at the end to hang the ornament. This ornament looks good with gold and silver yarn, too.

Garlands

Early settlers in America found both popcorn and cranberries growing wild. They made strings of both of these to decorate their trees. (You can also use other kinds of berries, like lingonberries.)

What you'll need: popped popcorn (cooled), fresh cranberries, needle and strong thread, scissors

Cut a piece of thread about 3 or 4 feet long (1 meter), and tie a knot at one end. Thread the popcorn and berries carefully onto the thread. Push it down to the end. When you fill up the thread, tie a knot in the other end. If you leave some empty thread at the ends, you can tie several strings together to make one great big garland. Hang the garlands carefully on the tree. If you're careful with them, these will last several Christmases. (Hint: make all-popcorn and all-berry garlands, or mix them up.)

Christmas Cards

Making your own Christmas cards is easy. There are lots of different ways to make them. One of the easiest is to save old cards from last year and just cut out the pictures. Glue them to folded construction paper, and write your own message on the inside.

To make your own Christmas cards from scratch, gather materials like construction paper, marking pens, paint, glue, glitter and sequins, cotton balls, bits of cloth and yarn, old magazines (to make collages from), and maybe a dictionary (so you spell the words right). Then let your imagination run wild. (Hint: you might want to measure some envelopes so you're sure the cards you want to send will fit.)

Christmas Treats You Can Make

Who doesn't love Christmas goodies? Here are some easy treats you can make yourself.

Frosty the Snowball

What you'll need: ice cream, grated coconut, aluminum foil, a cookie sheet, ice cream scoop, sprig of holly, small red candle

You have to work fast with this one so the ice cream doesn't melt. Cover a cookie sheet with aluminum foil. Scoop out big balls of ice cream onto the cookie sheet. Cover the ice cream with coconut. Cover the balls with more foil and put them in the freezer until they're good and hard. When you're ready to serve them, stick a sprig of holly or a candle in the top.

Extra-Special Christmas Punch

Here's something for when you're thirsty from all the Christmas excitement.

Have all the ingredients chilled. Mix together in a big punch bowl one can of grape juice or fruit drink, a one-liter bottle of lemon-lime soda, and an orange, cut in thin slices. The slices will float on the top. Add ice cubes to keep the punch cold.

Here's an old English poem that's easy to memorize. A ha'penny is a half penny, an old English coin. It's pronounced *hay-penny*.

Christmas is coming, the geese are getting fat,
Please put a penny in an old man's hat;
If you haven't got a penny, a ha'penny will do,
If you haven't got a ha'penny, God bless you.

O Christmas Tree

O Christmas tree, O Christmas tree,
How faithful is thy foliage
You keep your green and lovely glow
In summer sun and winter snow
O Christmas tree, O Christmas tree,
How faithful is thy foliage.

O Christmas tree, O Christmas tree,
You give us so much pleasure
At Christmastime we gaze on you
And feel great joy that thou art true
O Christmas tree, O Christmas tree,
You give us so much pleasure.

The Little Match Girl

by Hans Christian Andersen

This is one of the best-loved Christmastime stories of all, written by the great Danish author of fairy tales. Even though it was written many years ago, it helps us remember that, even today, there are many people who do not have a merry Christmas.

It was late on a bitterly cold, snowy, New Year's Eve. A poor little girl was wandering in the dark cold streets; she was bareheaded and barefooted. She certainly had had shoes on when she left home, but they were not much good, for they were so huge. They had last been worn by her mother, and they fell off the poor little girl's feet when she was running across the street to avoid two carriages that were rolling rapidly by. One of the shoes could not be found at all; and the other was picked up by a boy, who ran off with it, saying that it would do for a cradle when he had children of his own. So the poor little girl had to go on with her little bare feet, which were blue with the cold. She carried a quantity of matches in her old apron, and held a packet of them in her hand. Nobody had bought any from her during all the long day; nobody had even given her a copper.

The poor little creature was hungry and perishing with cold, and she looked the picture of misery. The snowflakes fell upon her long yellow hair, which curled so prettily round her face, but she paid no attention to that. Lights were shining from every window, and there was a most delicious odor of roast goose in the streets, for it was New Year's Eve—she could not forget that. She found a protected place where one house projected a little beyond the next one, and here she crouched, drawing up her feet under her, but she was colder than ever. She did not dare to go home, for she had not sold any matches and had not earned a single penny. Her father would beat her; besides, it was almost as cold at home as it was here. They lived in a house where the wind whistled through every crack, although they tried to stuff up the biggest ones with rags and straw. Her tiny hands were almost paralyzed with cold. Oh, if she could only find some way to warm them! Dared she pull one match out of the bundle and strike it on the wall to warm her fingers? She pulled one out. "Ritsch!" How it spluttered, how it blazed! It burned with a bright clear flame, just like a little candle when she held her hand round it. It was a very curious candle, too. The little girl fancied that she was sitting in front of a big stove with polished brass feet and handles. There was a splendid fire blazing in it and

warming her so beautifully, but—what happened? Just as she was stretching out her feet to warm them, the blaze went out, the stove vanished, and she was left sitting with the end of the burnt-out match in her hand. She struck a new one, it burnt, it blazed up, and where the light fell upon the wall against which she lay, it became transparent like gauze, and she could see right through it into the room inside. There was a table spread with a snowy cloth and pretty china; a roast goose stuffed with apples and prunes was steaming on it. And what was even better, the goose hopped from the dish with the carving knife and fork sticking in his back, and it waddled across the floor. It came right up to the poor child, and then—the match went out and there was nothing to be seen but the thick black wall.

She lit another match. This time she was sitting under a lovely Christmas tree. It was much bigger and more beautifully decorated than the one she had seen when she had peeped through the glass doors at the rich merchant's house this Christmas day. Thousands of lighted candles gleamed upon its branches, and coloured pictures such as she had seen in the shop windows looked down upon her. The little girl stretched out both her hands towards them—then out went the match. All the Christmas candles rose higher and higher and higher till she saw that they were only the twinkling stars. One of them fell and made a bright streak of light across the sky. "Someone is dying," thought the little girl; for her old grandmother, the only person who had ever been kind to her, used to say, "When a star falls a soul is going up to God."

Now she struck another match against the wall, and this time it was her grandmother who appeared in the circle of flame. She saw her quite clearly and distinctly, looking so gentle and happy.

"Grandmother!" cried the little creature. "Oh, do take me with you! I know you will vanish when the match goes out; you will vanish like the warm stove, the delicious goose, and the beautiful Christmas tree!"

She hastily struck a whole bundle of matches, because she did so want to keep her grandmother with her. The light of the matches made it as bright as day. Grandmother had never before looked so big or so beautiful. She lifted the little girl up in her arms, and they soared in a halo of light and joy, far, far above the earth, where there was no more cold, no hunger, no pain, for they were with God.

But in a corner by the house, in the early-morning cold, sat the little girl with rosy cheeks and a smile on her face—dead, frozen to death on the last evening of the old year. The morning of the new year dawned over the little body sitting over the matches, of which a bunch was almost burned up. She had wanted to warm herself, it was said. No one knew what lovely sight she had seen or in what radiance she had gone with her old grandmother into the happiness of the new year.

The Gift of the Magi

by O. Henry

In this famous story, American writer O. Henry has portrayed the spirit of giving at Christmastime perhaps better than any other writer.

One dollar and eighty-seven cents. That was all. And sixty cents of it was in pennies. Pennies saved one and two at a time by bulldozing the grocer and the vegetable man and the butcher until one's cheeks burned with the silent imputation of parsimony that such close dealing implied. Three times Della counted it. One dollar and eighty-seven cents. And the next day would be Christmas.

There was clearly nothing to do but flop down on the shabby little couch and howl. So Della did it. Which instigates the moral reflection that life is made up of sobs, sniffles, and smiles, with sniffles predominating.

While the mistress of the home is gradually subsiding from the first stage to the second, take a look at the home. A furnished flat at $8 per week. It did not exactly beggar description, but it certainly had that word on the lookout for the mendicancy squad.

In the vestibule below was a letter-box into which no letter would go, and an electric button from which no mortal finger could coax a ring. Also appertaining thereunto was a card bearing the name "Mr. James Dillingham Young."

The "Dillingham" had been flung to the breeze during a former period of prosperity when its possessor was being paid $30 per week. Now, when the income was shrunk to $20, the letters of "Dillingham" looked blurred, as though they were thinking seriously of contracting to a modest and unassuming D. But whenever Mr. James Dillingham Young came home and reached his flat above he was called "Jim" and greatly hugged by Mrs. James Dillingham Young, already introduced to you as Della. Which is all very good.

Della finished her cry and attended to her cheeks with a powder rag. She stood by the window and looked out dully at a gray cat walking a gray fence in a gray backyard. Tomorrow would be Christmas Day, and she had only $1.87 with which to buy Jim a present. She had been saving every penny she could for months, with this result. Twenty dollars a week doesn't go far. Expenses had been greater than she had calculated. They always are. Only $1.87 to buy a present for Jim. Her Jim. Many a happy hour she had spent planning for something nice for him. Something fine and rare and sterling—something just a little bit near to being worthy of the honor of being owned by Jim.

There was a pier-glass between the windows of the room. Perhaps you have seen a pier-glass in an $8 flat. A very thin and very agile person may, by observing his reflection in a rapid sequence of longitudinal strips, obtain a fairly accurate conception of his looks. Della, being slender, had mastered the art.

Suddenly she whirled from the window and stood before the glass. Her eyes were shining brilliantly, but her face had lost its color within twenty seconds. Rapidly she pulled down her hair and let it fall to its full length.

Now, there were two possessions of the James Dillingham Youngs in which they both took a mightly pride. One was Jim's gold watch that had been his father's and his grandfather's. The other was Della's hair. Had the Queen of Sheba lived in the flat across the airshaft, Della would have let her hair hang out the window some day to dry just to depreciate Her Majesty's jewels and gifts. Had King Solomon been the janitor, with all his treasures piled up in the basement, Jim would have pulled out his watch every time he passed, just to see him pluck at his beard from envy.

So now Della's beautiful hair fell about her, rippling and shining like a cascade of brown waters. It reached below her knee and made itself almost a garment for her. And then she did it up again nervously and quickly. Once she faltered for a minute and stood still while a tear or two splashed on the worn red carpet.

On went her old brown jacket; on went her old brown hat. With a whirl of skirts and with the brilliant sparkle still in her eyes, she fluttered out the door and down the stairs to the street.

Where she stopped the sign read: "Mme. Sofronie. Hair Goods of All Kinds." One flight up Della ran, and collected herself, panting. Madame, large, too white, chilly, hardly looked the "Sofronie."

"Will you buy my hair?" asked Della.

"I buy hair," said Madame. "Take yer hat off and let's have a sight at the looks of it."

Down rippled the brown cascade.

"Twenty dollars," said Madame, lifting the mass with a practiced hand.

"Give it to me quick," said Della.

Oh, and the next two hours tripped by on rosy wings. Forget the hashed metaphor. She was ransacking the stores for Jim's present.

She found it at last. It surely had been made for Jim and no one else. There was no other like it in any of the stores, and she had turned all of them inside out. It was a platinum fob chain simple and chaste in design, properly proclaiming its value by substance alone and not by meretricious ornamentation—as all good things should do. It was even worthy of The Watch. As soon as she saw it she knew that it must be Jim's. It was like him. Quietness and value—the description applied to both. Twenty-one dollars they took from her for it, and she hurried home with the 87 cents. With that chain on his watch Jim might be properly anxious about the time in any company. Grand as the watch was, he sometimes looked at it on the sly on account of the old leather strap that he used in place of a chain.

When Della reached home her intoxication gave way a little to prudence and reason. She got out her curling irons and lighted the gas and went to work repairing the ravages made by generosity added to love. Which is always a tremendous task, dear friends—a mammoth task.

Within forty minutes her head was covered with tiny, close-lying curls that made her look wonderfully like a truant schoolboy. She looked at her reflection in the mirror long, carefully and critically.

"If Jim doesn't kill me," she said to herself, "before he takes a second look at me, he'll say I look like a Coney Island chorus girl. But what could I do—oh! what could I do with a dollar and eighty-seven cents?

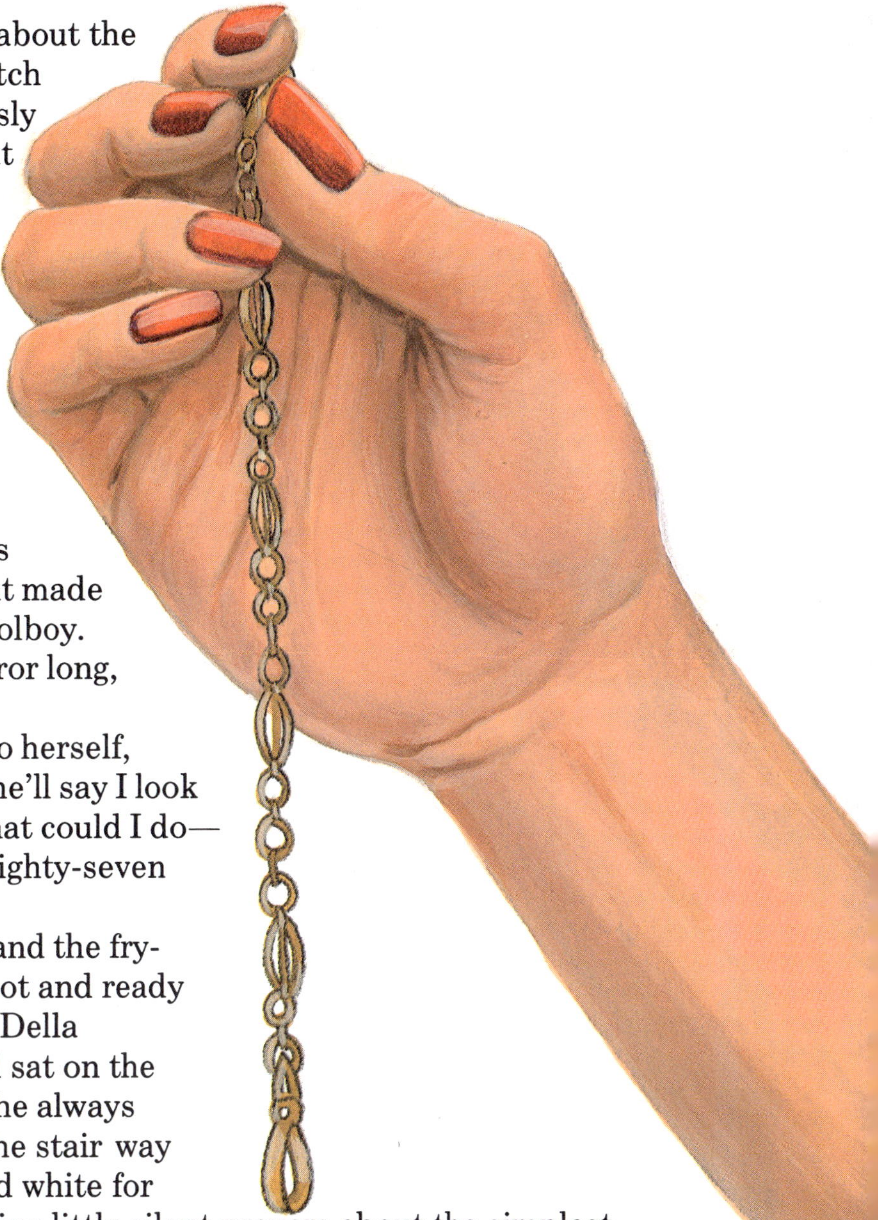

At 7 o'clock the coffee was made and the frying-pan was on the back of the stove hot and ready to cook the chops. Jim was never late. Della doubled the fob chain in her hand and sat on the corner of the table near the door that he always entered. Then she heard his step on the stair way down on the first flight, and she turned white for just a moment. She had a habit of saying little silent prayers about the simplest everyday things, and now she whispered: "Please God, make him think I am still pretty."

The door opened and Jim stepped in and closed it. He looked thin and very serious. Poor fellow, he was only twenty-two—and to be burdened with a family! He needed a new overcoat and he was without gloves.

Jim stopped inside the door, as immovable as a setter at the scent of quail. His eyes were fixed upon Della, and there was an expression in them that she could not read, and it terrified her. It was not anger, nor surprise, nor disapproval, nor horror, nor any of the sentiments that she had been prepared for. He simply stared at her fixedly with that peculiar expression on his face.

Della wriggled off the table and went for him.

"Jim, darling," she cried, "don't look at me that way. I had my hair cut off and sold it because I couldn't have lived through Christmas without giving you a present. It'll grow out again—you won't mind, will you? I just had to do it. My hair grows awfully fast. Say

'Merry Christmas!' Jim, and let's be happy. You don't know what a nice—what a beautiful, nice gift I've got for you."

"You've cut off your hair?" asked Jim, laboriously, as if he had not arrived at that patent fact yet even after the hardest mental labor.

"Cut it off and sold it," said Della. "Don't you like me just as well, anyhow? I'm me without my hair, ain't I?"

Jim looked about the room curiously.

"You say your hair is gone?" he said, with an air almost of idiocy.

"You needn't look for it," said Della. "It's sold, I tell you—sold and gone, too. It's Christmas Eve, boy. Be good to me, for it went for you. Maybe the hairs of my head were numbered," she went on with a sudden serious sweetness, "but nobody could ever count my love for you. Shall I put the chops on, Jim?"

Out of his trance Jim seemed quickly to wake. He enfolded his Della. For ten seconds let us regard with discreet scrutiny some inconsequential object in the other direction. Eight dollars a week or a million a year—what is the difference? A mathematician or a wit would give you the wrong answer. The magi brought valuable gifts, but that was not among them. This dark assertion will be illuminated later on.

Jim drew a package from his overcoat pocket and threw it upon the table.

"Don't make any mistake, Dell," he said, "about me. I don't think there's anything in the way of a haircut or a shave or a shampoo that could make me like my girl any less. But if you'll unwrap that package you may see why you had me going a while at first."

White fingers and nimble tore at the string and paper. And then an ecstatic scream of joy; and then, alas! a quick feminine change to hysterical tears and wails, necessitating the immediate employment of all the comforting powers of the lord of the flat.

For there lay The Combs—the set of combs, side and back, that Della had worshipped for long in a Broadway window. Beautiful combs, pure tortoiseshell, with jeweled rims—just the shade to wear in the beautiful vanished hair. They were expensive combs, she knew, and her heart had simply craved and yearned over them without the least hope of possession. And now, they were hers, but the tresses that should have adorned the coveted adornments were gone.

But she hugged them to her bosom, and at length she was able to look up with dim eyes and a smile and say: "My hair grows so fast, Jim!"

And then Della leaped up like a little singed cat and cried, "Oh, oh!"

Jim had not yet seen his beautiful present. She held it out to him eagerly upon her open palm. The dull precious metal seemed to flash with a reflection of her bright and ardent spirit.

"Isn't it a dandy, Jim? I hunted all over town to find it. You'll have to look at the time a hundred times a day now. Give me your watch. I want to see how it looks on it."

Instead of obeying, Jim tumbled down on the couch and put his hands under the back of his head and smiled.

"Dell," said he, "let's put our Christmas presents away and keep 'em a while. They're too nice to use just at present. I sold the watch to get the money to buy your combs. And now suppose you put the chops on."

The magi, as you know, were wise men—wonderfully wise men—who brought gifts to the Babe in the manger. They invented the art of Giving Christmas presents. Being wise, their gifts were no doubt wise ones, possibly bearing the privilege of exchange in case of duplication. And here I have lamely related to the uneventful chronicle of two foolish children in a flat who most unwisely sacrificed for each other the greatest treasures of their house. But in a last word to the wise of these days let it be said that of all who give gifts these two were the wisest. Of all who give and receive gifts, such as they are wisest. Everywhere they are wisest. They are the magi.

Christmas Carols and Poems

Here are a few Christmas carols and poems, some well known and some not so well known, that capture the wonderful spirit of the Christmas season.

The Twelve Days of Christmas

On the first day of Christmas my true love sent to me a partridge in a pear tree.

On the second day of Christmas my true love sent to me two turtle doves.

On the third day of Christmas my true love sent to me three French hens.

On the fourth day of Christmas my true love sent to me four calling birds.

On the fifth day of Christmas my true love sent to me five gold rings.

On the sixth day of Christmas my true love sent to me six geese a-laying.

On the seventh day of Christmas my true love sent to me seven swans a-swimming.

On the eighth day of Christmas my true love sent to me eight maids a-milking.

On the ninth day of Christmas my true love sent to me nine ladies dancing.

On the tenth day of Christmas my true love sent to me ten lords a-leaping.

On the eleventh day of Christmas my true love sent to me eleven drummers drumming.

On the twelfth day of Christmas my true love sent to me twelve pipers piping, eleven drummers drumming, ten lords a-leaping, nine ladies dancing, eight maids a-milking, seven swans a-swimming, six geese a-laying, five gold rings, four calling birds, three French hens, two turtle doves, and a partridge in a pear tree.

At Christmastime

A traditional English poem

At Christmastime we deck the hall
With holly branches brave and tall,
With sturdy pine and hemlock bright
And in the Yule log's dancing light
We tell old tales of field and fight

At Christmastime.

At Christmastime we pile the board
With flesh and fruit and vintage stored,
And mid the laughter and the glow
We tread a measure soft and slow,
And kiss beneath the mistletoe

At Christmastime.

The first Nowell the angel did say,
Was to certain poor shepherds in fields as they lay;
In fields where they lay keeping their sheep,
On a cold winter's night that was so deep.

Nowell, Nowell, Nowell, Nowell,
Born is the King of Israel.

They looked up and saw a Star,
Shining in the East, beyond them far;
And to the earth it gave great light,
And so it continued both day and night.

Nowell, Nowell, Nowell, Nowell,
Born is the King of Israel.

And by the light of that same star,
Three Wisemen came from their country far;
To seek for a King was their intent,
And to follow the star wherever it went.

Nowell, Nowell, Nowell, Nowell,
Born is the King of Israel.